Tidal Events

Mária Ferenčuhová

Tidal Events
—Selected Poems—

Translated from Slovak by
James Sutherland-Smith

Shearsman Books

First published in the United Kingdom in 2018 by
Shearsman Books
50 Westons Hill Drive
Emersons Green
BRISTOL
BS16 7DF

Shearsman Books Ltd Registered Office
30–31 St. James Place, Mangotsfield, Bristol BS16 9JB
(this address not for correspondence)

www.shearsman.com

ISBN 978-1-84861-574-8

ACKNOWLEDGEMENTS
'Threatened Species' appeared in the online journal *Asymptote*

'In the City of Dogs', 'Illuminated Cities' and 'Tidal Events' appeared in the
May 2017 edition of the online journal *Europe Now.*

'Heroes', 'Back' and 'Connection' appeared in *PN Review* 239

Contents

Translator's Note

Mária Ferenčuhová was born in Bratislava in 1975 and is a poet, translator and film theorist. She is editor of the of the film magazine, *King-Icon*, translates from French and teaches at the Academy of Performing Arts in Bratislava and the Academy of Arts in Banská Bystrica.

She has published four collections of poetry, *Skryté titulky* (Hidden subtitles, 2003), *Princíp neistoty* (Principle of uncertainty, 2008), *Ohrozený druh* (Threatened Species, 2012) and *Imunita* (Immunity, 2016), also a study of documentary film, *Odložený čas* (Time Delay).

Mária Ferenčuhová is in terms of her publishing history a wholly twenty-first century poet and this is true of her style, procedures and subject matter. With four collections in thirteen year she writes relatively slowly compared with some of her contemporaries considering that Slovak poetry collections are relatively slim volumes, usually much less than 1,000 lines in length. Slovak critics have characterised Mária's work as related to the ANesthetic generation and the Text generation of Nora Ružičková and Katarína Kucbelová whose neutral tone and use of abstract terms is in contrast to the post-Tender Revolution passions where an older generation of Slovak poets was able to release work energized by the Beats. Mária's work resists the pressure emerging from a still potent male-centred critical attitude to women poets which has confined them to a role where they wrote brief lyrics on intimate themes, nature or composed poetry for children. Despite the work of a number of strong, older women poets, for example Mila Haugová (born 1942), Anna Ondrejková (born 1954), Dana Podracká (born 1954) and Viera Prokešová (1957-2008), this expectation of a feminine as opposed to a feminist still poses a barrier to the reception of poetry by women in Slovakia so that poems whose energy and content is directed outside or beyond this patriarchal undercurrent often catch critics off guard.

The poet and critic, Ján Gavura, has coined the phrase "oko kameramanky" (camerawoman's eye), referring to her work as a lecturer on film. This is slightly misleading for Anglophone readers for whom Isherwood's "I am a camera" belongs to another era of realism in writing. Mária is not a realist in that sense at all. Part of a characteristic avoidance of using a poem to create a dramatic or emotional event for the reader is a resistance to possible reader expectation of the woman's poem, an expectation which ironically is often met by the anger in overtly feminist poems. Mária's strategies contain an ability to sidestep conventional responses as in the first poem in her first collection, In 'City of Dogs', where a decaying urban environment is rendered not in *grand guignol* gestures but in the details of leftover food, "smell cheese / fish and small stains on surface" and the hidden scuttling life of a city, "mice also quick: / underground. in colour. under seats." Judgement is deferred to the use of the second person "You pity the slow, everyone, who paused" and a sense of ceaseless, purposeless activity is evoked by the refusal to use capital letters at the beginning of sentences which are often telegraphic in structure. Such mimesis has remained a favourite device.

Mária's strongest work often seems to have urban origins. The trio of poems, 'City Maps', also from her first collection, continues using an unconventional punctuation and explores the distortions in perceptions of space that the city induces. These are taken up in 'Illuminated Cities' from her second collection and extended into sections where derelict individuals appear, where there is a switch to a temporary city of tents perhaps of refugees and in the next section motifs from the fatal infection of trees which is identified with the addressee of the poem. When the city becomes identified with parts of the human body containing a bourgeois family, "three children, four cars / and a pedigree dog" it is akin to the sensibility that Walter Benjamin analysed in Baudelaire in his essay, *Paris, the Capital of the Nineteenth Century*, especially in the section 'Baudelaire, or the Streets of Paris.' Illuminated Cities approaches an allegorical reading echoing the sense of submergence in Baudelaire's poems as in *Rêve parisien*, "L'enivrante monotonie / Du métal, du marbre et de l'eau," and the figure of the angel in 'L'Irrémédiable', "Au fond d'un cauchemar énorme / se débattant comme un nageur." In section 6 of Mária's poem the angel is the city who "indifferently offers a smile to the cameras" whilst distracted by "a lower trembling / tickling the soles of her feet, / after which hurtle packs of stampeding / rats."

The title poem, *The Uncertainty Principle*, has two fine Baudelairean lines, "By recollection in a single gesture of a demiurge / by which everything good turns to evil," but turns away from an isolated consciousness overwhelmed by the city towards personal relationships and carrying a child, "But even here grace comes: suddenly, from behind your back, / from within like the first movement of a child in your body." Personal responsibility preserves the individual from despair. "Yet it depends on me as to what I turn my face. / Whether to wind, sun or rain. / Or stones."

In her third collection there is an assurance in technique particularly in her handling of line in a poem, which enables Mária to broaden her thematic concerns. This has been commented on by a few Slovak critics as being too explicit although when I compare her oblique treatment of environmental issues and a poem featuring a Holocaust survivor with its Anglophone equivalents I suspect the survival of a critical habit from the days of censorship which tends to read everything into an image. However, Mária's poetry can effortlessly switch visual perspectives in the space of a single poem telescoping perspectives in an equivalent of the dolly zoom. In 'Threatened Species' the sequence opens with a view from space, "The view from above doesn't belong to a god / but a satellite", but by section 10 we have a microscopic viewpoint, "we examine the skin on faces / maps of blood vessels, craters for cells." Much of the phantasmagoric vision of the poem is akin to that of Elizabeth Bishop's poem, 'Night City', which carries the epigraph, *from the plane*. As with her earliest work there is also a merging of the self with the environment: human beings in this poem and elsewhere in Mária's work are also animals not separated from the environment. Often in her poetry the body becomes both exterior and interior landscape, a juxtaposition of macroscopic and microscopic vision akin to the hermetic doctrine of "as above, so below." The extension in range of thematic concerns is complemented by a wider emotional variety. 'Starfish' hints at a history extending back into the Hapsburg era and the devastations of the industrial and age and the Holocaust. There is an even more savage dismissal than in Philip Larkin's 'Not the Place's Fault' with her last lines in section 4, "Here, in this little town my great- / grandfather once owned a pub and a cinema. / He drank them up before they were taken from him. / A second-class station. / Our train doesn't stop here."

The sequence 'Poland' has a comic episode with a would-be seducer of the protagonist making a spectacle of himself and hurling an intended gift to the ground in disappointed rage. Indeed a broadening in the range of feeling that her poems encompass is evident especially when one reads her latest collection, *Imunita*, published in 2016. The section titled

'Key Indicators' (Kľúčové príznaky) is effectively less bound together thematically as in Mária's customary mode of working. The poems range from the horrific 'Inflammations' through the impersonal, 'Case History', to the visionary or hallucinatory, 'Connection', and sinister 'Something Could Have Happened' and 'Meteor' addressed to a six-year-old son with its unexpectedly tender conclusion, "Is the world so, as I see it? / Am I really / who I think I / was?"

With its ability to combine particular detail with visionary perception I read Mária's poetry with the same excitement that I first read the English Metaphysicals many years ago.

After many years of working with my partner, Viera, who prepared the base translations for our many collaborations on Slovak poetry this is my first venture into solo translation. However, Viera checked my translations as I went along and pointed out errors, as did Mária when I sent her the penultimate versions. I'm deeply indebted to both of them, and to the poet, Michal Tallo, who reviewed the final versions, for keeping me reasonably accurate and faithful to the original poems.

JAMES SUTHERLAND-SMITH

Tidal Events

Simply they've come out of the woods.
The whole herd slowly
setting out for the city,
Their hooves knocking
on the tarmac:
cars pull over,
they pour from the roads.

Roebuck and doe
have headed to the houses,
kneeling in front of gates,
folding their bodies on lawns,
pavements, roadway
and crossroads.
They bleat monotonously,
yet turn their heads away,
if someone wants to stroke them.

Every day
the new and new kind
lose their shyness.
They approach us,
look us in the eye,
lead us to the sea.

Without fear
together we stop to breathe.

In the City of Dogs

1.

Crystals grown too quickly to champ with teeth
scratch throat. with narrow fingers across
canvas voiceless retrace twists and turns.
local water next road: maybe according to old
secret recipe for a cleaning process to preserve
sludge. smell – survive survive, smell cheese
fish and small stains on surface: nothing
else, yet delicious food for dogs yesterday.

2.

mice also quick:
underground. in colour. under seats.
they seek food. between two trains.
utterly deafened: they follow – like you –
trembling wheels legs.

3.

last shells. from days previous. (cleaning
process to preserve sludge.) in darkening mirror
another of your faces.
each time belonging to a race they bewitch.

4.

you pity the slow, everyone, who paused,
showed palm and naked forearm, everyone
for whom private skin slid out from
sleeves much too much for eyes.
and if someone's random smile rests on you,
it stays random.
that which you wear under your hair
and here some so often address you
over-familiar.

5.

too long without measure: two three weeks like
different species. while they blinked, it died out.
Stumble against wall, forget in your guts.
this i: let it fossilize.
in Cuvier's museum simulating body with
spine in a crazy smirk.

City Map 1

can't convince cheeks of the importance of
of the wind hidden in a private cave, where its movement
is allowed to conclude.
unable to extract from the streets shrieking stares,
laughing with a loud hello at a stranger, ripping
an umbrella-gift from her hands.
Its breath incapable of sounding in the high libraries,
even in the reflection of blue glass soaring
in the space.
and not wanting to leave, because: up it goes only
(belly up) and only (head) down.
between is Sharp and Sour and Bitter. between is
a knock-out round there and back in weightlessness.

City Map 2

perhaps they're only running across this bridge pointlessly?
if here drab relentlessness triumphs as well, movement loses
sense and persistence gains it.
wholly unified: they wed on a starfish-graph
always in these fixed tracks: each time the same,
each time ahead.
and the bridge flips to its image.
foreheads break on sharp angles: in the same
rhythm as the rumbling metro that had long ago
occupied the diagonals.

City Map 3

a voice an angle to its echoes. Another pattern appeared:
freshly visible. The colours haven't changed, neither for me
has the previous colour been changed by today's.
and yet for this another arrangement of time, other dreams,
also another taste of water: i return to the city-patio
completely, slowly: unerringly through roofed
courtyards.

if they shouted yesterday, today they only whisper. nothing yet
do they blame. they still keep mum. In the city-patio neither wind
blows nor does it rain and the voice under low
ceilings does not multiply. here nothing has passed by.
but ships still arrive rounding
its southernmost tip.

Threatened Species

1.

A light green continent with a spiky peninsula
The sea, an emerald whitish interface:
The view from above doesn't belong to a god;
but a satellite.
A strip by the coast
the colour and shape of the Milky Way
an oil spill
silently expands.

In a new outfit,
brown and watertight
as a raincoat,
you hide a beak.
successfully concealing the essence of a bird,
you sigh finally
not like a seagull,
but a tapir.

2.

Leaning against the damp facade
with one leg draped over the other
and cheap cigarette in hand,
in a flood of green and then
in a white-brown dark.
You create the impression
you have befriended mammals,
birds and salamanders.

From here it isn't obvious that the animal portraits
are from a calendar.
Under the hat not even the sticky hair is obvious.
Thickening liver tissue is hidden under the skin,
night hides day,
laughter once more fear
and you drown a bleary glance
in thoughts transparent as alcohol.

3.

You possess. You have. It stays with you.
You save
the goods of this world in your palm.
You close it, open again
it's empty, you open the newspaper,
also empty, the radio
reporting a frontal depression,
road accidents,
outrages in distant lands.
you no longer see the forest
from the window, only the dull
house opposite.

4.

You should never have been born.
You weren't even inside properly.
You chose an inappropriate belly.
an improper father,
a wretched country.
You clawed your way out prematurely,
poking into matter, into the wrangle,
where they hadn't counted on you.

Then you hesitated. You almost didn't drop out.
They tugged at you with pincers, pressuring your temples
so strongly that since then only dark dreams
survive in them.

They tied you to your mother's back.
They showed you how to rip,
to bite,
to get under her skin.
They showed a direction
and then
without a word,
tripped you up.

5.

We didn't have to meet.
We could have clung on to all
the lives that little by little grow about us.
We could have calmly dozed into death.

But we tore down the nets,
redrew the boundaries,
shifted destiny, enlarged our holdings,
sowed new fields, demolished
monuments, built tracks,
buried the dead,
and the wounded we tended to so long
that at the end they remained with us forever.

6.

We ruined almost everything.
Moved it, deflected, broke, ground down,
stuffed it with rubbish, soiled it –
and now we fill in,
the shambles soonest
pouring in concrete.

7.

Certain folk also go out
in the streets on foot.
From under rotten planks,
from deep burrows and damp cellars
thousands of gleaming
eyes follow them mesmerically.

They still have not lost hope
of grasping, squeezing,
of any sort of rampage,
where they confirm a body count
and preserve their line.

8.

All these children.
They run among the lights
and disappear under the gate.
In piles of dry leaves
they steer clear of traps. They zigzag,
come out as dark falls,
sort out paper after paper,
folder after folder,
they smoke cigarette butts,
drink up wine, sip milk, juice,
curl up under cartons,
cover themselves with branches.
Calmly they wait
until the time comes for them.

9.

(And then silently
occupying abandoned sites
the young whelp
in depopulated neighbourhoods,
without surprise they explore their bodies.
armour on their chests, shiny healthy gums
jaws full of transparent saliva,
which burns holes in plastic bottles
and changes alloy to porridge.)

10.

We do not give up. Carefully
we examine the skin on faces
maps of blood vessels, craters for cells,
noting trembling hands, stuttering,
cracks in sentences.
As others measure pressure and sugar,
we measure the level in thinking.

When two hands can't clasp together,
there's a space still remaining between words.
We fill it with understanding
the way others stuff windcheaters with quilting.

11.

Yet how many must still take to the streets,
how many times must the mechanical dance be repeated,
so we notice our eyes,
our grimaces are alike?
How many times a day must the temperature jump
about twenty degrees up and then back down,
so we understand that to dress
for the weather is no longer enough?

In the wind flow, in the fast moving
clouds, in the front of cumulonimbus
loaded with drops of heavy water
and adorned with plumes of ice crystals,
we unwittingly return to magical thinking.

But at once after the balance of the horizon the rope of logic
is stretched linearly, pragmatically,
without understanding anything but personal consequences.

12.

It doesn't take much: touch the earth
like one's own skin,
let the nervous system
overgrow through the border of the body
take root,
descend to the depths of the river,
not to persist in running,
to stop,
give.

13.

Annoying slowness, laziness
masked by masses
of fundamental decisions,
steps forward, sideways, back,
short circuits and procrastination,
all of this has only to delay the clarity of perception.

At least for a while
carefully watch the destruction,
at last with a clear awareness
that you don't need us,
you never have,
only we you.

14.

Rivers gradually excavate new beds.
Cobwebs will tremble, too, for a while
above the roofs of
buildings. Sludge dries, seals the windows.
Coasts, freshly cut out
on the borders of a new country,
shine first of all. Then
the ocean scours
with multi-coloured debris,
fragments and panels.
Finally beaches
appear
with gray or brownish
sand.

15.

And what about you?
Will you have the body like I remember?
Or joints, segments. Compound eyes – will you have eyes?
Will you send signals or use speech,
encode messages and toil
towards meaning?

Gravity and other forces
on my surface will create
figures.

Will you be able to read them?

Illuminated Cities

1.

Summer does not depart, remains as inflammation on stale roads.
hot stone, not even traces of steps (and yet moist air);
wounds do not heal, the same movement every afternoon – wiping
dust with a hand from your eyes and oil from the scorching wheel. October.

Not even a return: enduring in the gaps – the city does not remember,
neither do you want to: numb footsoles, chapped hands, why not confess –
alley, passage, the street discloses from behind the corner instead of (another)
memory. Next. Likewise.

And on a platform a madman, completely shabby
(nobody is scared of him any more), the transfer station Réaumur Sébastopol:
at the very top a man is asleep in his socks,
from one a bandage sticking out, but only a few dare to cover their nose.

Behind a window without blinds someone is getting drunk,
all alone, behind a window with a blind I do my face,
I don't air the room, quietly I set the phone,
and finally fall asleep.

2.

Finger code, noise, secret entrances, angry with yourself
for recklessness (in the first moment) for reasonableness (in the second)
and resenting the solitude – what virtue? In terms of eternity
it's all the same, whether in this world alongside this body
(or with another), in terms of the moment: vote emptiness. And wait.

Old woman, not really old, rather already burnt up, perhaps senile
and perhaps deranged from the year dot, rides up and down the elevator,
greets the world at large, repeats aloud, "Yes, yes" to the numb,
with an obliging expression says to everybody "Sir, Madam",
and touching the cheeks of children with her fingers.

With a skewer to the belly, to another a word to the heart:
quarantine, forty days of silence.
Flame, cellophane, a scorched idea
you infect the whole colony by yourself and you wonder
when they'll condemn you.

3.

There are houses made of wood, plastered or just canvas pasted on,
carpets instead of walls, in the corners cables, in the cracks dust
and wind under the door.
An instant boil kettle, microwave, double cooking plate,
whoever sleeps,
doesn't move. Follows the meanders, doesn't detect that on the banks
there's no green, doesn't notice pavements, continues further,
to where they ride a camel,
with a rucksack on their back,
where grey blocks of flats stand in the sand only they gleam,
as in the suburbs,
and under the windows tents,
a fountain without water and the sky in flames,
you want to return to the river, there's no way,
– not in a dream, and therefore not at all –
and it's enough to open your eyes, run along the walls,
burning carpets, acrid smoke
barefoot without aprons:
these stairs
still standing.

4.

They said that the treatment of the trees would absorb
a tenth of the budget and would not be effective.
The disease spreads from the Balkans,
it remains there unrecorded,
and therefore they've agreed to felling without protest.
They've opened a vertical steel space,
a glass palace, they've protected themselves with light that
by degrees penetrates up to the dark
uncontrolled areas,
expelling parasites purifying mycelia,
if need be isolating it from the healthy core and
not allowing infection.
The labyrinth of cold light
smooths faces, removes their features
and with a sharp finger points at the sick.

5.

Shifting under the surface of the road, by submerged river,
vena cava places, on the banks drying out
the foundations of dwellings, filling cracks
with one's own warm body,

with a working tool like an extended arm
catching more fortunate lives:
bourgeois families, three children, four cars
and a pedigree dog.

In slow motion installing the seals,
dams for the elements,
and secretly leaving in them a reserve
at least for a single saucy hair.

Returning during the night
capillaries of urban circulation
and humbly waiting as long as the other
untamed world does not awake.

6.

Suddenly it is here:
in whole flocks
they tumble down headlong
like fossilized birds.
the wind blowing their writing, ash
in hair, cooling pavements,
soft and cosy,
full of splinters and rubble, broken bodies.
The closed arms of the built over earth:
with eyes covered with a band of glass wool
she indifferently offers a smile to the cameras
and in the general hubbub silently
focuses on a lower trembling
tickling the soles of her feet,
after which hurtle packs of stampeding
rats.

7.

     Witness of, not survivor of.
Every perception remains under the skin,
You press, it hurts: you know where you have to press.
Phantom pain
       hurts just like the real.
Travelling in large machines, yielding to their mercy
       and only then feeling fear.
       Walking around cities.
You know where you have to go. You know where to look.
       Only rarely do you talk about it.

Nevertheless

Nevertheless he was
also in our family one,
whose head burned likewise
outside only cold skin and dry hair.
and at the same time he stopped at nothing.

He left in me much,
much was washed out,
and his life lived on in mine.

Often he injured his brow,
and what later dropped away from me
for that matter was also almost killed on the stairs,
almost crushed its head:
this head often burned, too.

Then it went.
I had thought that it would be forever,
but it went, bodies gradually broke up
shattered, the innards disintegrated, decomposed,
only a shell remained

I entice death to it,
even if it doesn't want it,
honouring its memory.

Stupor

1. Logorrhoea

The day will come when child'll want to hear the tale:
for instance, about the people of the valley of the river Var,
future lovers
sauntering along the old gray path
under bloody rocks and
the louring mountain sky,
that just before the storm
falls on the path
on the very next bend.
And when they stop by the stone church
and on the terraced square they embrace fiercely,
everywhere they're at home.
They eat fish for lunch and supper.
lie down in the parental bed,
all day swim in the sea
and their bodies are
brown and smooth,
flexible and scaly
dry and old,
until at length they crumble like the rocks
towering over the road
into bloodbrown dust
and blend with the landscape.
Colour remains only a memory
like a postcard from a nearby resort.

Or a tale
of the interior, of a city of the plains
by quite another river, of the angular buildings
with a faded roof, with broken gates
and gutters, which twist away from the walls.
Where water runs down the render and window frames,

people persistently standing at the entrance
to department stores,
offering twigs of trees, bear garlic, hawthorn,
a dog-eared dictionary
bits of privacy and
god-bless-you.

Where on the streets several cyclists
tremble two entwined hands,
a mane of hair in the wind and cars everywhere.
Crowded, overheated trams
and passengers with plastic bags,
who have long wished to get off.

Or at least a tale
of a long night road
and large, serious eyes behind a window,
which wait for whether they'll see somewhere
an actual real horse.

2.

The fact remains stark:
they make a hole in the stomach,
pull out the fetus.
suture, clean, plaster over,
weigh and measure.
they bring and show,
leave.

In a few hours
they administer drugs
checking blood pressure, womb shrinkage,
catheter,
change the sheets, underbedding,
bring the child, remove her again,
leave.

Where the body ends, life begins.

Where passiveness begins,
death does not reach today.

3.

There is no time for dreams nor for stories,
The body is tired, flows of blood, milk,
scattered attention.
broken up perception,
cleft awareness.
a tree with three roots and
shapeless trunk,
leafless arms –

yet I know where I was happy,
museums, pavements, squares,
underground galleries, steps and touches,
reflections of faces, a gesture over water,
shoulder to shoulder in perfect harmony,
patience, humility, diligence,
freedom in solitude,
an immense borderline.

Disintegrated memory
debris in the air,
glitter,
particles of pollen, rain,
if only to find
in a mighty outpouring an embrace,
which does not belong to me,
or even you.

4.

The only solitude is silence.
A unique freedom falls quiet.
Constricting walls, angles. A pure white
emptiness.

To leave a particular, tangible life:
to become oneself again.
without extension,
without continuation,

without future.

5.

Training ends:
everything in the impure. Drawings, sketches,
projects of posthumous masks
messages of goodnight, fear before travel,
a drink, washing my face
and suitcase in my hand
or at least twine.

To clean quickly.
To prepare the scene for the photograph.
To wipe the dust.
Another dream is only a desire for solitude.

Silence:
And one more.
For a second, for all eternity
this tiny hand I won't take away from my face.

6.

An oval slit in a dark place,
a detail, on which it's necessary to focus:
an eye with its slanted corner
leads to the face of the originator,
pest (Father),
a mirror image of the impossible
in the out of shot field.

in sound
a wailing infant afflicted with colic
a vertical tone, which disintegrates bone marrow,
trepans the skull and consumes cells
with toxins of defencelessness, superimposed images,
burns the retina, magnifying glass under the sun
rays on the palm,
sore medallion,
a box with treasures.
feet in dry leaves,
warm colouring
with long sleeves
and rolled down:
us.

We touch each other with faded hair.

7. Amenorrhoea

And yet ...
Yours is.
To be blessed.
Come.

Till the end of time.

Meteor

We prepared a terrible death for you.
We left you to brawl with wild beasts.
We thought you were one of them.
We let you parry fangs with milk teeth,
claws with the shells of your soft fingernails.

Our prolongation,
pink thread
tangled up in life
a ball of hair, tendons
and pliable bones.

In the middle of a man-made
rain-forest needing water three times a day
so it won't change in the wilderness,
from what it's been until now.

A calm unobtrusive moment
of entanglements. A leap to silence
only millions of cicadas
rhythming.

The last reflections of a six-year old:
who cuts off the sun,
even when it's burning,
who never gets tired
pushing it over our heads?
Who drifts meteors
across the sky?

Is the world so, as I see it?
Am I really
who I think I
was?

Something Could Have Happened

Sometime around July the ninth
I stopped distinguishing what was real…
I told them that I didn't know what had happened.
That something could've happened that I don't remember.
Incidentally, what I remember is dull.
Scraps of quite ordinary things:
dog hair, muddy water,
time knotted.

When they pushed back the cupboard, I saw
the door behind it: it didn't fit,
it was metal and warped below.

Then I realized that the photos
glued to the bottom of a drawer
I hadn't put there.
Neither was the manuscript probably mine.
I saw that behind the door
was another staircase and another door,
behind which lived those,
whom I'd encountered
in the cellar.

When I turned round,
men in uniform no longer stood
in the dark apartment, she stood there,
as though she had always been there, the whole time.
Had I done something wrong?
Had they done something wrong to me?
At the end of the corridor the mirror swung out

seven times.

Before Departure

1.

I have long been patient.
Calmly wrinkling into the paving
adhering to the ground.

Footprints,
spilt juice, hair, crumbs,
broken crayons, battered toys,
bronchitis, eczema, allergy.

Passed away. Erased. Covered over by another.
Free radicals, bites,
flashes, stings,
proboscises,
antennae,
hairs,
segmented legs,
claws,
suckers,
compound eyes,
webbed wings,
light spectrum,
rainbow.

Adhering to the paving
I wait for the train to come.

I open the door to the balcony,
I focus on the city noise
slowly try to lift my leg –
and it obliges.

2.

We're silent as two balls of yarn.
Your wrinkles are extensions of mine,
we signal with gestures:
placing a cup on the table
meaning to invite to dance
the hand that grips the cup,
put it in the sink,
ruffling the air,
starting to descend,
stumbling on something hard, an elbow,
finger, so perhaps on to your chin and open mouth,
that suddenly appear at the level of my shoulders,
waiting for a smile and would have gained it,
had I got up, taken the cup,
placed it in the sink,

but I sit.

3.

Even after ten years
I forget that the unsaid
reaches you but rarely.
The medium may be a touch or a glance,
but more often it is not.

Even after ten years
I remember that
better than travelling by train
is the idea of travelling by train
and better than solitude
is now only the idea of solitude.

4.

In the winter garden,
there where the wall is wettest,
the plaster crumbles.
I sniff, I pick at it with a finger,
at length lick.

Starfish

1.

While I'm packing again
you learn my itinerary by heart
and connect the points on the map.
Yellowish cigarette butts
moisten between the blades of grass,
ladybirds, sloe bugs and winged ants
that attack from the back
and land in your hair.
You leave with a hoe
going to dig into the earth, thinking
that you lead a life deeper than mine.

Each departure is definitive,
each arrival is a new beginning.
Vainly do you impress in your head
railway routes,
etch a starfish in your brain,
you won't find me
although I haven't gone away
from you.

2.

I travel with Magda.
I imagine a clean,
fragrant dresser.
Flowering cherry.
Duvets. In a basket, bread.
Above Magda unmoving,
icily limpid eyes
and on the sheet a hair:

in an overexposed, distorted memory,
once they would be silhouettes equally fragile
as our present limbs upholstered with cracked
skin, as if we banged
our backs painfully in an open carriage
and overhead the last rockets
shimmer for us, which will soon fall
to the wounded earth.

3.

Finally home.
The first person you meet,
is wearing a Sunday suit of your father's.
The door's open,
faces not.
Where have you been living? Nothing's changed.
And yet the Four Towns, your home,
smelt otherwise.
Restoring furniture and repainting the walls
is not sufficient. Washed quilts, bleached tablecloths,
everything impure ironed out except you,
except for the
wrinkle above your nose.

4.

A hilly landscape
devastated by industry,
coughs up bloody mucus, with a yellowish-gray
beard, smoker, that from the world
desperately hides mining towns
with reservoirs like drops of dew
in the leaves of Lady's Mantle.

On the plain only the aquapark gleams
and abandoned cotton factories,
blind dusty windows,
not even children playing in their ruins.
The light brown Vah poured out.
On its waves broken branches,
gaudily white swans.

Here, in this little town my great-
grandfather once owned a pub and a cinema.
He drank them up before they were taken from him.
A second-class station.
Our train doesn't stop here.

5.

The last dead factory.
Masonry has long since given in.
Greenery grows out of it.
Insects have undermined foundations,
surviving in the cracks
and feeding birdlife.
Only now
is the rough construction
truly done.

Note: *"The Four Towns" refer to four towns in Eastern Slovakia, Kežmarok, Poprad, Spišská Nová Ves and Levoča, which were free towns in the medieval Hungarian empire.*

Poland

1.

The wide Vistula with desolate banks
and the bridges all at once so far apart!
Poplars, aspens, hornbeams,
gravels and a heavily gray sky
intense, in major mood,
adult you return home
in an air-conditioned carriage,
in cool pastel attire.
Gradually, through the window you scrutinize cracks in stone
– weathered concrete –
and in the construction efforts
(stadiums, skyscrapers, HQs and possibly
even apartments) you already see doom:
it's sufficient that the train has crossed the river
and rails corrode,
the sleepers break like decalcified teeth
landscape exposes a prehistoric skeleton
a creature of the recent present
and an ancient childhood monster.

2.

Country: memories.
Chewed up by railway tracks,
platforms, ramps, scarred by embankments,
the past here shows itself as a chthonic phantom
directly from the grass between the stones.

3.

We didn't go far enough.
Yet right here the present time ends.
Unmarked platforms,
broken stairs,
trains, where first class is one heated compartment
in the second class carriage.
The seats whiff of naphthalene,
and yet fleeting contact with their surface
opens old wounds.

Against the flaring sentiment
you are protected by your clear thinking.
Do you glance at your shoes,
feel embarrassed,
hope you haven't just thought
that you belong to the same species
as these mute fair-haired men,
that with their knees together
travel in beige trousers
and with blue glances
indifferently look through you?

Really, are there so many small dead
factories in this country?
Really isn't this train stopping in a field?
The guard doesn't answer, but in the course of an hour
he comes three times to check your ticket.

4.

Yes, this man got off at Lublin
Solely on account of you, although he had elsewhere to go.
With just the one shirt he directed his steps there,
and never stirred. He bore up when you left him
standing in a strange city, content that at least he'd got a look at you.
He sold spare parts for buses,
didn't pay taxes, seemed to be ready to cheat on his wife
even choosing gifts for yours, not his young children.

But this one who held out a hand to you,
implying touch and then offered you
a pot full of blooming geraniums
(you demurred and he with savage cry
hurled it on to the middle of the road),
made a spectacle of himself.
A lift, a maze of emergency exits swallowed him,
a neon hotel night froze him.

So finally you always end up in intimate self embraces,
your limbs calmly aligned with your torso,
and with a face above you which, with a little luck,
a god could wear
or death.

Back

Everything seems to be okay.
In the Lublin yeshiva rabbis study once more,
although the Jewish Quarter
they left razed to the ground.
The trains go more or less on time.
We can rely on the announcements or the arrivals of taxis
and underground passages
cave in only once in a hundred years.

The smelly couchette has been almost inoffensive for me
and looking at the ancient
enormous sleeping cars with curtains
I'm even happy.
I settle down opposite a Girl Scout
in a synthetic skirt. Ah, on its edge
a steam iron has printed, a visible point
and obvious rows of dots.

Half asleep, I can't make out
whether sometimes behind my back
an enormous bottom has sat down on the seat
or if the train has finally begun to move.
I am astonished only
that storks really nest on chimneys
or on tall poles
exactly as in fairy tales.

Heroes

1.

Insufficiency of sleep, surfeit of meanings,
On the fenders grime. Dust.
A firework display of puddles and clay
glowing wheels,
a dark head behind the steering wheel,
golden in the child seat.
Uncertainly they leave the family network,
they bear away everything of consequence,
everything, from which for years
you spun your own tale,
although you always craved for something else.

2.

Like strings you draw your vocal cords from your throat.
You unpick your cheeks, from under your hair you pluck
your cranial cap, tighten the skin like a tent
all over the gutted apartment.
You cover it up, with your vocal cords you darn
and put yourself into a single tone,
in which weeping is not heard
and finally sleep can germinate in it.

3.

Implosion.
A face from which protrudes only cheekbone and nose.
An angled back bending under beams:
What burden do you carry again on your shoulders?
The horizon consists of outstretched hands.
By legs empty buckets
and foreign children.
They assemble a mosaic
from shattered make-up.

4.

A single impulse suffices. A photon
strikes steel.
The tale turns on its heel.
I'm sorry, but it scoffs at heroes.

Tales

1.

In the twilight between ribs
an exhalation.
A false sound.
Worn out, leaky pipes,
A contorted chest
with shadowy arcades.
Once slashing pain
determined their arches,
today air hissing in them.
And over the ruins of the body flurries
of indole. Jasmine. Sandalwood. Moss.

Lying in the same position
as a Dresden cathedral:
with knees directed skywards
and a gutted belly full of rubble.

In the meantime the child lives,
slowly, inexorably grows.

2.

Cheer me up, mama, he says.
today a smile has burst from me
and all day long slipped from my mouth like knickers.
Cheer me up properly.
Spindly back, grazed knees,
all afternoon from the pavement on the beach front
his fingers sweeping the sand
and wondering if he really wanted
to sink boats or better to build them.

3.

In the nervous movement of the ears,
in protective colouring,
in saliva trickling from the mouth
and a second later a monkey's leap,
in the tail of the scorpion, in the sticky lanolin
of a ram's fleece I find my image
outlined with awkward
pre-school children's hands.

Whatever way have I travelled,
into whatever trap have I dived,
however have I dried my hair in the sun
to achieve exactly this form?
A pattern of behaviour can be
determined by family backgrounds,
with the tone of late night whispered stories
or quite ordinary silence.

4.

Here, in the hand,
on the throat,
a throbbing artery
awaits for the opening of crossings.

Here, this road and this car,
rail tracks, birds, and this tree
will be in a few moments
regrouped material.

Here you set the aperture,
the exposure time.
Now sit here
and skulk.

The Uncertainty Principle

1.

In plain light of day two or three objects thrown to the ground,
pots, boxes – things in which other things are stored,
pure composition – a mess: nothing must remain on the ground.
You fend off evil with minor rituals.
You go back three times to check the lock on the door.
Soles of your feet between two cracks, exactly there and not
        elsewhere.
Breathe to the east, don't think,
across the edge, into the chinks, hidey-holes, sums on your fingers,
with little steps through the whole zone.

In the particular world the rate of abstraction fluctuates.
With your mouth you outline the words "pen, knife, matches".
How to organize them?
According to the purpose, sharpness, danger?
According to colour, hardness and complexity?
And why just a pen? Why not wood, paper, glass?
Or skin, fissure and spit?
You know that it's necessary to abstract, but you've got no idea
what comes first.

2.

Suddenly we're here.
mirrored symmetrically
like trains passing each other in opposite directions
(they draw out strange stories across dirty suburbs
to empty bistros, where men in berets
sip evaporating beer
and women forget their gloves, lipstick, compacts,
photos of their own children,
sometimes keys,
cards with phone numbers,
tickets for the bus,
but tickets for the theatre usually not).
We are here, opposite each other,
derailed from
the only way of joining as a collision.

3.

Dosing, pumping out luck from brass vessels
and waiting while it dries: a museum exhibit with a matt patina.
Looking from behind the glass, not thinking.

Pouring water (muddy to clear)
With our hands' dry skin rubbing a surface to a shine,
not breathing – waiting.

Breath,
water.
Fruit.

Entirely at the edge of consciousness, where dreams scream
          incoherent sentences
about fear and guilt, yet we still believe that the world cannot be
organised poorly.

Passive. Overloaded with acts,
by spinning head, pendulum movement of our feet,
chest forward and back,

totally cursed.
By recollection in a single gesture of a demiurge
by which everything good turns to evil.

4.

You don't get by with dailyness – passing the days,
working, holding on to life, running to God
only in moments of fear: it isn't enough.

Autumn, slowly daybreak,
face, cheek leant against wood.
solitude, unavoidability, excuses.

But even here grace comes: suddenly, from behind your back,
from within like the first movement of a child in your body,
and only briefly.

The desperate don't dream. Their sleep is
a dark cave,
momentary redemption.

5.

We met
and we stayed together:

a door deviating while running,
in the dark a fleeting touch of fingers
indirect, immodest –

another driving parallel without overtaking.
In cities. Each to their own.

Together everyone alone
and yet together
at length a noble ideal of romantic love
in much too small an apartment.

Deservedly.
Evidently like breathing.

Like sleep.
Like family.

6.

Nothing is obvious.
Neither learnt patterns of behaviour,
routine shots of traffic accidents,
every time the same creased sheet.
Facial expressions. Tears, laughter.
The changing seasons of the year.

Only yesterday I walked round
lakes behind the city indifferently.
Today, I can see death in them.
Yet it depends on me as to what I turn my face.
Whether to wind, sun or rain.
Or stones.

7.

Once more you do the same.
With an outstretched hand you drive away of your own accord
rapidly flowing air.
You calculate, you look for signs
a twisted leaf, an abandoned house,
a lame bird.
which every morning flies to the window and
waits for bounty.

What at all do all of those do
whose face is screwed up in pain
because of you?
You want to guess from your palms,
what your errors will bring,
for the only chance is
to join hands and wait with hope.

Attractions

1.

I lost my speech.
Only my eyes remained open
and mind drawn to the story.
Plots of visual themes:
obscenely exposed in shop windows
jewellery bought in pawnbrokers
across the country,
cut flowers, stems rotting in a vase,
fingers oscillating over the keyboards
of a cash register
the dirty bodies of workers
obscenely exposed
to a roasting sun,
mosquito larvae in a tank,
jewellery in a vase,
dirty fingers,
larvae in a roasting sun,
workers across the whole country,
bodies in a tank,
themes drowned in words
left to the mercy of an assemblage,
to fast track actions,
one image combined with another,
a whole new meaning precipitated:

floats on the surface,
or sinks to the depths…

2.

You won't get away. You've already damned yourself a hundred times.
Useless. The skin on your hands cracks
just as your lip splits exactly
in the middle of a sentence. It follows
the grain of your pores. The stressed areas of the body.
Parchment. You exfoliate the outermost
Layer. You don't fool your pores.
You still just don't get
what you have to learn.

3.

Milestones: education,
fear. And then responsibility.
Only for a moment keep an eye on a multitude
of wrong decisions
and then consider,
on what basis to evaluate them
as wrong.

Pain, disappointment, is there a segmented line instead
of a straight one leading from nowhere to eternity?

4.

You hunt recklessly for the tale of golden earrings:
poignantly on black velvet.
To redeem from captivity.
To take charge. To master.
Golden studs in your ears:
suddenly you're nobody.
Your reflection in the mirror
is of interest to nobody.
Not even you.

Case History

Her father died at 37 years from heart disease,
her mother lives, her son healthy, history
from a psychiatric point of view
unremarkable.
Common childhood illnesses,
not under treatment, takes no medication,
seven years ago a stomach operation:
internal injuries after being stabbed with a knife.
Casual employment. Otherwise waitress.
She lives alone, in a hostel, smokes 10 cigarettes a day,
drinks 2-3 litres of wine per week.

At dawn a neighbour found her
on a balcony half-naked
leant over the railing
shouting that at last the time had come.
She is conscious,
communicable,
disoriented,
uses bad language.

After 14 days of hospitalization
stabilized, mood lucid,
excellent response to medication.
This morning released
to outpatient
care.

Connection

She woke up connected
to a lit fibre,
penetrating her head
at the highest point on the crown,
purifying inside,
flushing out sludge
destroying pathogens
and repairing tissues.
It spread through her fingertips.
She changed plastic to gold,
at sight ennobled
the people, society,
various races.
News of her power
spread by the ether
almost by itself,
she healed at a distance, but also
by touch,
each according to choice,
she saw how the filth gradually
leaves bodies
enters the earth,
warms it.
They discovered her after years
burnt to ash
in a house of which only
the outer walls stand today.
Below them huge reserves
of fossil fuels
are rumoured
to be hidden still.

Inflammations

I have in my body inflammatory processes.
Especially in the veins and in the lymph nodes.
My joints swell, I read that it can be
gout or rheumatism.
In my body feelings stagnate.
They are strong.
Every situation calls forth a reaction in me.
I do not regret the past.
I have every feeling all at once.
There is nostalgia, regretting,
there is still a great passion,
for everybody.
There is anger here, also even envy,
a strong prickling in my heel,
a contracting of my left ventricle.
I cannot stand up on my legs,
I bear weight on my toes.
My arch has fallen. At first the cruciates and then
The arch between toe and heel.
The blood in the veins of my calf presses on the valves,
the blood wants to return,
a vein bulges.
A ligament has been unable to keep my intestines in my belly,
also my stomach bulges.
I have in my stomach all my feelings,
toxic substances,
I have mercury in my brain.
Sometimes it presses into my eyes,
their corners shine from it.

Sometimes I have mercury on my tongue,
my lips grow heavy,
occasionally they billow out.
I do not want to smile.

Sometimes I'm so full,
that I open all the folds
with sharp objects,
I emit toxic gases,
I cut my perineum
and grease pours out of me.
I'm alone with this weight.
Everyone is in me,
in my insides,
but they say nothing.

Profile Picture

In hospital seclusion
apparently I'm not alone.
On the screen words of support.
I almost don't breathe from emotion.
Liquid crystals in my eyes,
and in my lungs it constantly rains.

Not even the earth could drink in more water.

The last photo,
in which my face
becomes an aquapark
(transparent tubes for toboggans
emerge from my nose,
others sink into my veins,)
will be relevant forever.

if I dare
post it online,
if I were just
able to move a finger.

Forecast for Tomorrow

25.5.2012

Drizzle, rain
with stormy locales.
Afternoon in the west
diminishing cloud
and institutional flurries.
Early evening fatigue.
In rare cases fear,
a stiffening in a cloud of uncertainties.

9.7

As if the hospital
had become a little bit further
from the city every week.

Who lives so close to the track?
They, their wives, their children
stored on balconies
bicycles, laundry hung out,
men's underpants, T-shirts.
from the train a boy's T-shirt
looks like his underpants.

The stinking have been moved on.
To the east. High in the north.
The sick to where?

16.7

"Hi, where are you?
What are you doing?
Are you alive?"

6.8

In the treatment ward
comfortable armchairs
as in a hairdressers,
talks about the weather,
politics
and new drugs,

while it fills,
some read
a book, have a nap,
eat a snack,

perhaps even within the hour
they will void
everything.

13.8

Under the scar behind the bone:
obey,
sit quietly.

Overhead gray, clouds sopping.

The first drops will lick the sweat from my face
and the earth sucks all the others down.

20.8

Don't explode,
don't blossom,
don't shake,
don't fall apart,
don't send through your bloodstream
reports to other organs,

don't make things up, sit,
today,
in a week,
in a month,
a year

and every other Monday.

8.10

Healthy.
My head
as the first breathes in the meaning of the concept. My body
tries to follow the thought, to repeat gesture, strengthen
its muscles, to transform a fatty wrapping to parchment:
my body heaves itself up.
Gradually reducing doses,
breathing this,
this,
this
moist air!

19.11

Nevertheless.
At first speech.
Words began to peel off things.
Day after day. Stickers on the skin
of bananas. I can't remember the meaning of the words
"basket", "brush", "there"
I don't know where exactly "there" is
The variety of signs astonishes me,
yet I don't know, whether my head causes this uncertainty
or whether it's due to language.

26.11

She's moved.
A few days ago,
the clouds changed shape ever more quickly,
she revived
began to grow
accelerated her heartbeat, sharpened
her breath
not attention.

24.12

We shouldn't have reduced the dose of medication.
We shouldn't have
lowered our faces
before the gusts of the north-east wind
and waited for the sun.

25.12

What is it, this yellow behind the window?

31.12

This
       stitched up   look
in the mirror,   in the window
in the eye   in the pit   in   in
in   i-i-i-in   in
my face
i-in
in
       i i-i-i in

my hair
once

                                    true
hair   in my eye i-i i i in   ba-
                    a baseball cap!

1.1.2013

Light.

You don't know what it is any more,
but you still ask for it.

www.ingramcontent.com/pod-product-compliance
Lightning Source LLC
Chambersburg PA
CBHW022200080426
42734CB00006B/522